This Book Is M
With Love By

_____

_____

_____

For

_____

_____

_____

By

Zulanda Publishing

When were you born?

_____

_____

Where were you born? Tell me more about it

_____

_____

_____

_____

_____

_____

What was your house like as a child ?

Were you named after a family member or does your name have a special meaning ?

Did you ever hear any stories about anything interesting that happened during or soon after your birth?

Do you have a nickname that your siblings or friends call you? How did you get the nickname ?

What were the full names and places of
birth of your parents and grandparents?

Parents;

Grandparents;

Could you tell me a story or a special memory about your parents and grandparents?

Parents;

Grandparents;

How many children were in your family? What are there full names?

Could you tell me a story or a special memory about your brothers and sisters?

Brothers;

Sisters;

How did your family spend time together when you were young?

Did you ever have a Family game night?

_____

_____

If so, what games would your family play?

_____

_____

_____

_____

_____

_____

What kind of car(s) did your family have when you were growing up?

How were those cars different from the cars today?

What would you and your family do when the electricity in your house went out, when you were a child?

What is the most important lesson that your parents taught you?

Did your family ever take holidays together?

_____

_____

What was your favourite holiday that your family ever took?

_____

_____

_____

_____

How often did your parents read to you?

_____

_____

Did you ever play any tricks or pranks on your parents or siblings?

_____

_____

_____

_____

_____

How did your parents discipline you?

On what occasions would you get new clothing or new outfits?

How often would your parents take you to get new shoes?

Who would baby sit you when your parents weren't home?

_____

_____

_____

Who was your favourite baby sitter?
And why?

_____

_____

_____

_____

_____

Can you tell me about our family history,
And the family tree?

What do you appreciate most about your parents?

What is the earliest memory that you have?

Who was your childhood best friend?

What is diferent about growing up today than when you were a child?

What is the most surprising thing you enjoy about being a child?

Did you like or dislike moving?

Can you remember all the different places you lived, and what years or dates you moved?

Did you have a bed time?

If so, what time did you have to be in bed by?

How old were you when this bed time was enforced?

What was your favourite movie you ever saw in your childhood?

What was the first movie you ever saw?

How often did you see movies at the theater, as a child?

When did you learn how to swim? Where did you go swimming as a child?

Did you ever go for hunting or fishing as a child?

Do you remember the day when you learned how to ride a bicycle?

Did you like to read books, as a child?

_____

_____

_____

How often would you read?

_____

_____

_____

_____

_____

What was your favourite books to read, as a child and why?

Did you ever run away or hide from your parents after you had done something wrong?

Did you ever get into a physical fight with another child?

What was the worst injury you ever got,
as a child?

How did your parents react on the injury?

What is your saddest memory from childhood?

What is your happiest memory from childhood?

What is your scariest memory from childhood?

What is something that you were just never able to understand, as a child?

What is the funniest thing you ever remember saying, as a small child?

How did you celebrate birthdays in your family?

What was your favourite or most memorable birthday gift you ever received, as a child?

What was your least favourite type of
birthday gift to receive, when you were little?

How did you celebrate Thanksgiving in your family?

How did you celebrate on Christmas day in your family ?

How did you celebrate New years' Day in your family?

What was the first school you attended?

What were your favourite subjects in grade/ Key stage school?

Did you play any junior sports in grade/ Key stage school?

Did you play any musical Instruments in a band during grade/ Key stage school?

If so, which ones?

Did any of your siblings or cousins go to school with you?

_____

_____

_____

If you had siblings or cousins that went to school with you, what classes or school activities did you participate in with them

_____

_____

_____

_____

_____

What was one of your favourite class field trips that you took?

Which advise can you give to a student who is still at school ?

Were you ever disciplined by a teacher or sent to the principal's office?

_____

_____

_____

If so, what happened?

_____

_____

_____

_____

_____

_____

How often was your school delayed or cancelled due to snow or other inclement weather?

Were there any subjects or teachers you disliked particularly liked or disliked? Why?

Who was your best friend in high school ?

How would people who knew you in high school describe you?

Did you work during high school ? If so,
What did you do? If not Why didnt you ?

What did you do after high school ?

Where was the farthest away from home that you ever traveled, before your 18th birthday

How were your next door neighbours like?
friendly, mean, sociable, etc?

How often did your family or next door neighbours visit each other ?

Did you ever get troubles as a child or teenager? Did you have a curfew and what time was it ? Did you ever miss curfew ?

Did you ever have low points as a teenager?
How did you get through it ?

Tell me about a leader who impacted your life for good when you were a teenager ?

Who were your friends from school what did you do together for fun ?

Did you do any sports or clubs when you were a teen? If so what are your favourite memories ?

Do you remember any words or sayings that were common in your youth that nobody says anymore or very rare ?

What was the biggest thing you ever got in trouble for ?

What pets have you had? Tell me more about them

What is your favourite place you have ever visited and how was it like ?

What is the longest trip that you have ever gone on ? Where did you go ?

What is the most beautiful place you have ever visited and what was it like ?

How did you fall in love ?

How many times have you been in love ?

Who was your first date? How long did you date?

How did you meet my mum/ dad / Grandma /Grandpa? Tell me more about that?

How did you know that it was the "real deal" ?

How often did you go for dates? How was it like ?

What advise do you have on love and marriage for couples today ?

Where was the first place you lived away from home? Do you have any crazy roommates stories?

What is the best christmas or birthday gift you have ever recieved and given?

What is your favourite thing to do on the weekends?

Did you ever get really sick or have to go the hospital? What happened?

What was your first job?

_____

_____

What was your first car you drove?

_____

_____

Where was your first home out of your parents house?

_____

_____

_____

What are your top five best memories?

What lessons would you like me to learn from your experiences growing up?

Notes

Notes

Notes

Notes

Notes

Notes

Notes

Notes

Printed in Great Britain
by Amazon

47836884R00059